THE FLYING ARTIST'S GUIDE TO
PASTELS

First published in 2005 by
SpiceBox™
1627 Ingleton Ave.
Burnaby, BC Canada
www.spicebox.ca

Text Copyright © Philip Berrrill 1996
Written and Illustrated by Philip Berrill

ISBN 10: 1-894905-92-x

ISBN 13: 978-1894905-92-3

Printed in China

Photography by Peter Raymond, Southport

CONTENTS

About the Author:
Philip Berrill
"The Flying Artist"

Philip Berrill is a professional artist, art tutor, lecturer and author whose techniques and methods of learning to paint are taught and enjoyed worldwide. Born in 1945 in Northampton, England, Philip now lives in Southport with his wife Sylvia and daughter Penelope. When asked how he first embarked on his career path, Philip recalls the tale of how he discovered paint at the age of three. It was one sunny afternoon that Philip wandered into his father's glass greenhouse in their backyard and saw at the far end a large bucket of whitewash and a tubular pump sprayer. Being naturally inquisitive, Philip loaded the sprayer with whitewash from the bucket and had a lovely afternoon spraying all his father's best tomatoes and plants white. By the time his father returned to find his son and the entire inside of the greenhouse dripping with whitewash, Philip had discovered that with paint you could change the world.

By the age of 14, Philip's enjoyment of art at school, where he studied under the Welsh artist and tutor, John Sullivan, helped him decide to make a living as a professional artist. Philip held his first one-man exhibition at the age of 18 followed by other group and one-man exhibitions. At the age of 28 a major exhibition of his work was held at Liverpool University and as a direct result of this exhibition Philip realized his ambition to become established as a professional artist. He launched his very successful art classes using his special approach to teaching, sketching and painting. These classes proved so popular Philip went on to develop his worldwide correspondence art courses. In the 1980s Philip embarked on the next stage of his career that lead to his nickname "The Flying Artist". After offering highly sought-after painting holiday courses in Great Britain, additional tutoring and painting holidays in Europe were then organized in wonderful locations such as Rome, Venice, Florence and Paris. Subsequently Philip

was invited to lecture and demonstrate painting on sea cruises around Europe and visits followed to Houston, Dallas and Dubai. Philips exhibition "The Italian Connection", an exhibition of his sketches and paintings of his Italian journeys and other European locations, has been very well received.

Philip's love and enthusiasm for sketching and painting is infectious. He believes that art should be for everyone and that you are never too young or too old to start sketching. Philip's students have ranged from 10 to 80 years of age and he continues to enjoy passing on his enthusiasm and knowledge of how to sketch and paint, gained over 30 years, to people from all walks of life and almost every background imaginable. Philip's sketching and painting courses and techniques are designed to be suitable for people of all abilities and all ages, and he has over recent years found

Philip Berrill painting during a 12-hour painting marathon session he did for a television telethon.

4

great enjoyment in the challenge of producing his own art videos. These videos led to the invitation to produce and present his own 13 part television series, "Paint with the Flying Artist" and this project in turn has led to the writing and illustrating of his own series of art books especially for you. These books, *"The Flying Artist's Guide to..."* are designed to cover a wide range of mediums, techniques and subjects to introduce you to the joy and pleasure of sketching and painting. Each book has been beautifully presented in a high quality laptop easel with all the materials you will need to get started painting and drawing. The compact form and portability of each kit will allow you the freedom and spontaneity to capture each moment of inspiration the way Philip demonstrates with his own work.

We hope that you will enjoy the *"Flying Artist's Guide to..."* kits and that they will assist you in your journey of sketching and painting.

Right: Philip Berrill sketching a statue

Bottom: A pastel study by Philip Berrill

Introduction

Have you ever stopped to watch someone create a picture with colored chalks on a sidewalk, or perhaps while on holidays have had artists offer to sketch your portrait in black and white or colored pastels? If so, the chances are that you, like myself, have had your interest captured by the medium of pastels.

Many people will think of watercolors, oil painting and sketching when considering a new art medium to explore, and pastels have, for quite a number of years, fallen to the wayside. Sometimes a medium can drift out of fashion, only to be rediscovered by a future generation when it gains a new and fresh popularity and I am delighted to say that pastels are once again becoming a popular medium of artists, students and leisure painters. I often find that particularly teenagers, whose concepts of art are not yet firmly fixed, are usually keen to explore all art media forms and will often have an immediate feel for pastels. Most adults think in terms of the traditional mediums of art and still I quite often notice that when adults attend one of my pastel courses for the first time, they are surprised that they have overlooked pastels and enjoy the versatility of the medium.

Part of the joy of working with pastels is their potential for picture making because they offer scope for the individuals' freedom of expression and style. Pastels lend themselves to the rendering of almost all subjects and are robust and durable, especially if due care is given to storing or framing the finished work. Pastels can be gloriously messy, but by taking the appropriate steps, pastel pictures can be produced with remarkably little fuss or mess. Pastels are an ideal medium to use at home, in a classroom or in art studios because they require few supplies, are quick to clean up and store, and the materials occupy so little space, that they are convenient to carry with you outside on sketching and painting expeditions.

Pastels are easy to learn to use, and this book and kit is designed to introduce you to the widest possible range of pastel techniques as quickly as possible. With the supplies in your kit, and by following the demonstrations I outline you will be able to catch the essence of a subject with just a few strokes of a pastel and produce a preliminary sketch as the basis for a main picture as well as produce finished pastel pictures. If you are a beginner, this is a splendid medium to start with. If you are a painter, but have not tried pastels, I feel confident you will enjoy the experience when you try them. If you already use pastels, this book will introduce you to some new ideas and approaches to the medium and will help you develop your skills still further. I hope that through reading *The Flying Artist's Guide to Pastels* they will weave their charm on you, and that you will spend many enjoyable hours exploring this captivating medium.

Above: Soft chalk pastels in various colors

Students, Jane, Sheila and Nathaniel, members of one of Philip Berrill's art classes, watch as Philip gives some finishing touch advice.

Pastel Materials and Equipment

Pastel Materials and Equipment

One of the great joys of pastels is that not only is it an inexpensive medium, but you can start with the minimum of materials. While pastels and paper are all you'll need to begin immediately, you will want to start adding materials to your collection over time that suit your personal preference. The following description of pastel materials will give you a full understanding of what is available and I will also suggest other items you may want to gather to add to your pastel kit right away.

Soft Chalk Pastels

Soft pastels are made from a mixture of very fine pigment, chalk and pipe clay mixed with water. They do not deteriorate with age and the finished painting will not crack, fade or darken over the years. Soft pastels usually come in round stick form and are soft, powdery and are applied directly to the paper. Delightful effects can be achieved by gently rubbing one pastel color on top of another. Pastels can commonly be obtained individually or in sets of 12, 24 or 48.

Firm Chalk Pastels

Firm or hard pastels usually come in square stick form and are essentially chalk based and are ideal for pastel drawing, pastel sketching and detailed work where a firm confident line or detail is required. These firmer pastels are less smudgy than soft round pastels, and while they can be blended by layering one color on top of another, they do not lend themselves so readily to blending with the finger. Picasso, Degas, Delacroix and many other great masters of the past century have used this type of pastel, which can be obtained individually, or in sets of 12, 24 or 48.

Pastel Pencils

Pastel pencils are firm or hard pastels encased in wood, in the same manner as the traditional graphite pencil. Pastel pencils are useful for the artist wanting to make more detailed studies but where the velvety pastel look is required. The point of the pastel pencil can help give the detail more easily. Animal and bird studies, in which the effects of fur and feather are important, are good examples of subjects often

rendered in pastel pencil. Most artists collect a mixture of soft, hard and pastel pencils as they can be intermixed.

Oil Pastels

These are quite different from the chalk-based pastels I describe above, and should not be confused with them. Oil pastels are made from a combination of pigments, oils, and wax as a binding agent. They provide a sharper, more defined look, unlike the softer, more powdery chalk pastels. They are more difficult to blend, but they also allow for other interesting techniques.

Pastel Paper

The soft and powdery nature of pastels means that they need a paper with a slight texture, or tooth, to enable the pastels to grip the surface, not a paper with a smooth or shiny surface. Some pastel techniques, especially the pastel sketching technique, allow the background color of the paper show through, and thus become an integral part of the whole picture. For this reason, pastel paper comes in a wide range of colors and is produced by a wide range of art paper manufacturers. In pastel painting technique the whole surface of the paper is usually covered, which of course means that the color of the paper is less important.

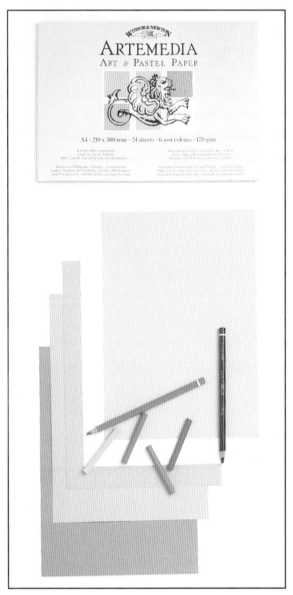

It is possible to use colored construction paper (the type used in children's crafts) for trying out ideas and pastel sketches. It is quite inexpensive and a pad usually has a range of colors to experiment with. However, for finished and important studies, be sure to use proper pastel paper otherwise the quality and color of the paper will deteriorate over time.

Pastel paper comes in sheet, sketchpad and sketchbook form. When you are purchasing replacement paper, be sure to look carefully at the colors in the pad to ensure that they are colors you feel you will be comfortable working on. A selection of white, pale blue, pink, and pale gray is good to start with. Try to ensure that your pastel paper is at least 60 lbs or above in weight, this will ensure that it is substantial enough for you to work on. An ideal weight is 80 lbs.

Mistakes, Erasers and a Brush

There will be occasions when you make a mistake, or you decide that you would like to change part of a pastel picture. Do not try rubbing out the area with a normal eraser; the pastel will smudge and look unpleasant. To correct an error or to make a change, use a dry, round paintbrush with fairly stiff bristles. Gently jab at the area to be changed until it loosens and dislodges the surface pastel. Blow this away from the picture and then use a soft kneaded eraser to remove the remainder of the pastel. The item, area or passage of work can then be reworked.

Fixative

When the pastel picture is finished there is always a risk of it being smudged accidentally. A clear fixative is often used by pastel artists to hold the loose particles of pastel to the surface of the picture. Fixative normally comes in "ozone friendly" aerosol cans and is very convenient to use in this form. It can also be obtained in bottle form with a tubular mouthpiece to apply a spray of fixative. Alternatively, some artists prefer not to fix their pastel studies as they believe the picture loses a little of its freshness. The choice is a personal one but I do recommend that you start with an aerosol fixative.

Boxes and the Care of Pastels

Loose pastels can become soiled and grubby as color is transferred from the sides of one pastel to another in their box or with your fingers. One suggestion for storing pastels is in a shallow, plastic storage box with a press on lid approximately 9" x 6" x 3". Line the box with a stiff piece of netting so that the sides come almost up to the top and half fill the box with ground rice. If you place your soft pastels in the box on top of the netting, and then snap the lid on and lightly shake the box, the pastels will bury themselves in the ground rice, which will keep them remarkably clean. The sides of the netting can then be pulled upwards to bring your pastels to the surface when you wish to work with them.

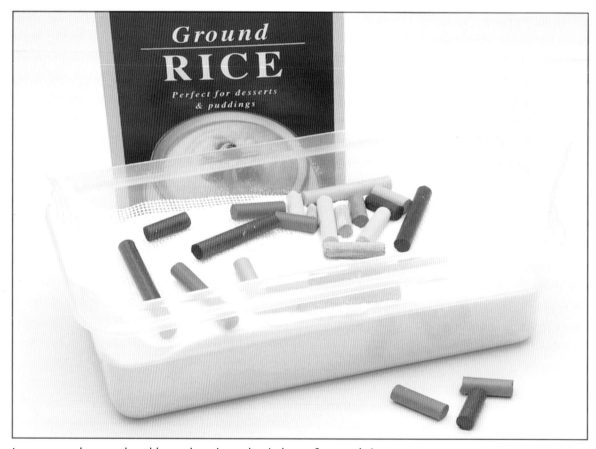

Loose pastels stored and kept clean in a plastic box of ground rice

Drawing Board

Many people like to work flat on a table, while others prefer to stand and work at an easel. In either situation, you will require a rigid surface on which to work. The surface will need to stand the firm pressure that you will often be applying when you work with pastels. A compact, portable easel can be a good purchase, as it allows you a lot of versatility in working outside or in various locations. You may put a bulldog clip or a little adhesive tape along the edges of your paper to secure the loose end so that it doesn't curl up.

If you take a page out of your sketchpad to work on or buy paper by the sheet, you will need a good drawing board. These don't need to be expensive and can be obtained from most art supply stores. Drawing boards are made from laminated wood or white plastic-covered chipboard. Do not use drawing pins, use drawing board clips or masking tape to hold the paper to the surface.

Newspaper

For some artists, a drawing board can be too firm a surface to work on. The soft, cushion-like effect when using a pastel sketchpad can be quite pleasant. If you want to create the same cushion effect, lay 10" x 12" sheets of newspaper on your drawing board before fixing your sheet of pastel paper on top.

Portfolio

Pastel pictures should be kept clean and flat, ideally in a portfolio. To ensure that one pastel picture does not transfer color to the back of another one in the portfolio, I recommend that you cut a piece of greaseproof (wax or parchment paper) paper the same size as the picture. Use a paperclip at each corner to fix the protective greaseproof paper to the pastel study.

Drawing board

Drawing board with newspaper

Pastel and drawing board

Easels

Table easels can be very helpful and practical tools. They can be set at different angles and can be folded flat for storing, which makes them very versatile. However, you can also purchase table easels that can be set at different angles and can be folded flat for storing which can be very versatile as well.

If you wish to purchase a sketching easel, test a few different models at the store to ensure that it can be positioned for working standing up or lowered to sit at, as well adjust to a table flat position. It should be light enough to carry, yet rigid enough to work on, leaving both hands free to hold and work with the pastels. It should also collapse to be compact and easily transportable.

Sundry Items

I recommend a few other items you may want to pick up at your art supply store. A 2B pencil, a fine, black felt-tip or nylon-tip pen, a stick of charcoal and a small sketchbook for notes, ideas and practice are all items you will find useful to keep with you. A small block of fine grit sandpaper and a craft knife will assist in shaping the ends of your pastels, and a kneaded eraser, and a firm bristle, round paintbrush are ideal for removing mistakes. You will also want keep a small can of fixative for using on your finished pictures. You may also want to keep an eye open for a carry bag with compartments for the additional materials you start to acquire, and a portfolio for storing your completed art.

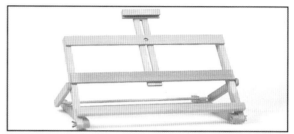

Table easel

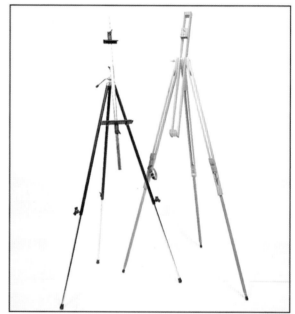

Sketching easel

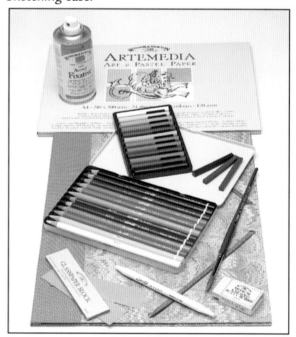

Various materials for pastel drawing and painting.

Demonstration 1
Pastel Strokes and Pastel Marks

Play with the pastels to see how many effects you can create. Take a brown pastel, snap it into three pieces of differing length, short, medium and long. Take the medium piece between your thumb and forefinger and with the top edge of the pastel make long, medium and short downward strokes on a light-colored paper. Try hatching, or a series of parallel lines. Try crosshatching, where you make hatching lines and then cross other parallel lines over the original lines in a different direction. Jab the pastel at the paper to create dots, also known as stippling.

Hold the pastel so that the long side of the pastel is touching the paper. Lightly pull the pastel down the paper. Make long, medium and short side strokes. Now do that again with a lot of pressure from your hand and fingers on the pastel. The tone of the pastel stroke will be quite dark. Carry on down the page using a little less pressure, which should give a medium tone, or strength, of the pastel color.

Pastels shown broken into pieces

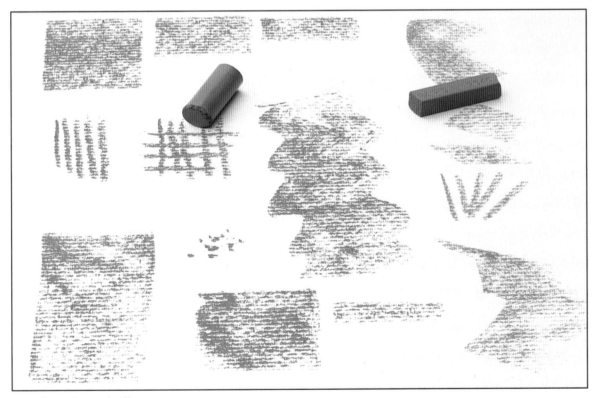

Pastel marks and effects

Demonstration 2
Shaping Pastels

Pastels come in varying degrees of softness or firmness depending on the manufacturer, from very soft to quite hard. Pastels that are soft, but a little firmer than the very soft pastels allow you to shape the ends offering scope for even more types of marks and effects.

In the photos to the right and below, I show how, with a craft knife, you can carefully shape round and square pastels to a point, or to a chisel-edge. Sandpaper can also be used to help shape a pastel end, or to resharpen the right-angled edges of the sides of a square pastel if they are worn away with use.

Experiment with the top edges, sides and shaped ends of your pastels to see if you can create effects and marks in the way I show below.

Handy Hint: To prevent pastels from smudging they should be spray fixed. Details of how to do this can be found on page 62.

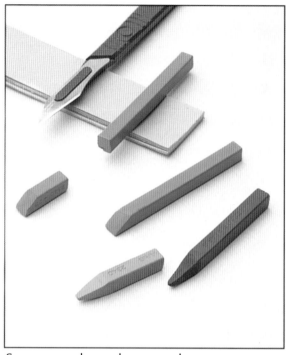

Square pastels - end you can shape

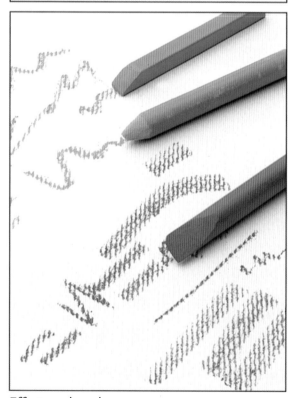

Effects and marks

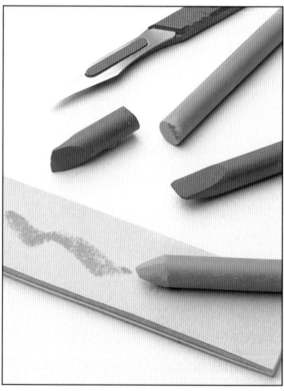

Round pastels - flat and pointed end

Demonstration 3
Using Black and White Pastels on Gray Paper

The dramatic and wonderful effects pastel can create are achieved with the minimum of materials. Here we look at the use of white and black pastel on gray paper. We use the white to identify the highlights and the black to identify the darkest shadows. The gray paper acts as the medium, or third tone.

Right: Take a piece of white pastel and draw the wineglass shown here.

Below: Now draw the glass again putting in the white highlights, then add the black pastel. Likewise try the saucepan, the shiny metal bowl and spoon, then the candle and candlestick holder. Don't let the black and white pastels mix on the paper when trying this demonstration or the resulting color will be gray.

Look around your home for similar articles such as teapots or coffee pots, cups and saucers, mugs or ornaments you could try to sketch using this technique.

A white on gray study

Handy Hint: Have a strong source of light shining on the objects from the left or right. This will help emphasise the highlights and the strong shadows.

Black and white pastel studies

Demonstration 4
Still life: Black and White Pastel

Let's stay with the black and white pastels on gray paper, and progress from single objects to a still life composition. The group consists of a wine bottle, wineglass and bowl of fruit set against a pink drape and standing on a checked tablecloth.

Stage 1: I normally suggest a subject is sketched in light outline with white pastel or a 2B pencil. This ensures the subject is correctly drawn and provides a sound foundation for your picture. Many pastel artists like drawing in the way seen here. Use the side and top edge of your pastel to shape the objects. Using the side of your black pastel, lightly add the tone of each item you see, including the background drape and the tablecloth.

Stage 2: The light is coming from the right side, so the darker tones and shadows will be on the left of the objects. Using a little extra pressure on your pastel, add the medium tones to those areas.

Stage 3: Still using the side of the pastel, add the darker tones to the drape and wine bottle. Now use the side and tip of the white pastel to add the highlights. Finally use the top edge of your black pastel to draw in the line and details of the fruit. Use stippling (dots) to create the effect of the orange skin. Add the line and details to the glass bowl, wine bottle, wineglass and tablecloth.

Stage 1

Detail

Stage 2

Stage 3

Demonstration 5
Landscape
Black and White

For our last black and white demonstration we'll think about the outdoors and progress to a simple landscape. The subject consists of a pathway leading to a cottage, with trees to the right and distant trees, a lake and hills beyond the cottage.

Stage 1: Sketch the subject with a 2B pencil. Using the side of a piece of white pastel, sketch in the white of the sky, sunlit lake, highlights on the trees, cottage, fields, fence and path.

Stage 2: Using a piece of black pastel, add the pale and medium tones to the hills, trees, roof, path, fields and fence.

Stage 3: With the top edge of your black pastel, pick out the detail of the stonework on the cottage, right-hand trees, path and fence.

After you complete these first demonstrations you may be surprised at how much control and dexterity you are beginning to achieve using just two pastels. This work provides an excellent foundation for your future pastel sketching and painting.

Stage 1

Stage 2

Stage 3

Handy Hint: With landscape subjects, the paths, roadways, hedges, rustic walls and fences can be useful to help lead peoples eyes into the picture.

Demonstration 6
Venetian Bridge: Monochrome

Stages 1, 2, 3 and 4. With the pastel sketching technique, the color of the paper used can play an important role in the overall look of the picture. Here I use a cream pastel paper with a sanguine, reddish-brown, square pastel. Hold a medium -sized piece of the pastel with its side flat to the paper, and, in the centre of the page, make a sweeping upward curve for the under-side of the bridge. Add the softer tones to the left and the right of the bridge opening and the darker stone slabs of the top of the bridge. With downward strokes add the first tones of the buildings and with angled strokes add the canal walls.

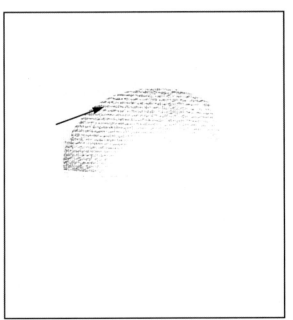

Stage 1

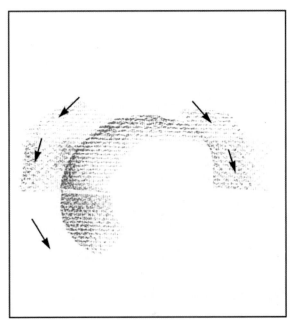

Stage 2

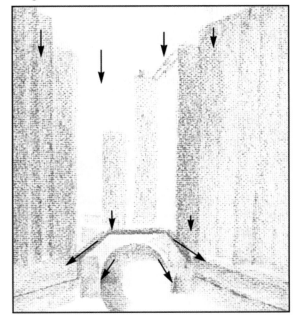

Stage 3

Stage 4

Stage 5. Continuing with the side of the pastel, but with a little extra pressure and with shorter strokes, add the start of the windows and shutters. Using the top edge of the pastel, pick out the more distant windows, the edges of the roof tiles and the lines denoting the stone slabs on top of the canal walls.

Take great care not to let the side of your hand, wrist, shirt or blouse sleeve catch and smudge the surface of your pastel picture.

With the top edge of the pastel, add the lines and detail to the windows and shutters, church, bridge railings and canal walls. Finally a few sweeping lines on the canal will give the reflections of the canal walls and the bridge.

Stage 5

Finished study

Demonstration 7
The Doorway: Pastel Study

Now is an ideal time to begin using some of the many wonderful colored pastels you will find in your pastel set. Doors and entrances often make excellent subjects, so let's start there.

Stage 1: Use a piece of white pastel to block in the main shape of the door, doorstep, pavement and potted plant.

Stage 2: With the side of a piece of yellow pastel, block in the front door. With the side of a piece of white pastel hint at the white painted wall. Using a gray pastel and a ruler add the lines on the door and a hint of gray in the glass window above the door. With green and brown, block in the potted plants. Use a gray pastel on its side to block in the path.

Stage 3: Use the top edge of a black pastel just to outline the top overhang of the door, the detail in the windows and the overhang supports to the left and right of the door. Use a ruler and a dark brown pastel to carefully add the lines for the four door panels. Pick out the outline of the step in gray. Use a little black to suggest the edges of the paving stones. Pick out the darker green and darker browns of the plants and pots. Add the door knocker, letter box and door handle. The colored pastel study is now finished.

Stage 1

Stage 2

Stage 3

Demonstration 8
Sunflower

Pastels allow artists to produce very delicate or very bold work and give freedom for individual styles. In this demonstration I deliberately selected black pastel paper as I knew that the yellow, brown and green of a sunflower would look very striking against it. (Use a piece of black construction paper for this demonstration.)

Stage 1: Draw the sunflower outline in yellow pastel. The leaves and stem should be drawn in green.

Stage 2: Fill in the petals with yellow. On this occasion the black outlines add to the very dramatic style of the picture. Put a little green on the central circle, then stipple reddish brown and black pastel to develop the striking centre of the flower. Use a light and medium green for the leaves and stem.

Stage 3: The leaves and stem can have the line and detail added with yellow and black pastel. The sunflower can simply be left with the contrasting black background or a background of your choosing can be added. I have put in the blue sky. Be adventurous, experiment and play with ideas and images.

Colored pastels used

Stage 1

Stage 2

Stage 3

Demonstration 9
Pointillism

The French artist, Georges Seurat, developed a technique of painting pictures using dots of paint, known as Pointillism. In this demonstration I have used the candle and candlestick holder from one of the earlier demonstrations to practice this technique.

Stage 1: Sketch the subject out lightly using white pastel.

Stage 2: Stipple the white candle with dots of gray in the areas away from the flame. Using first yellow, then orange, then red and then mauve pastel, stipple the candlestick holder and candle flame in the way shown in the Stage 2 panel. Use white, then yellow for the highlights, then light and dark blues for the color of the background drape and its shadows.

Stage 3: Use yellow, light green and dark green for the tablecloth. Use dark green and black dots under the base of the candlestick holder. I have shown the three stage build-up of the main features of this picture in the detail panel.

Stage 1

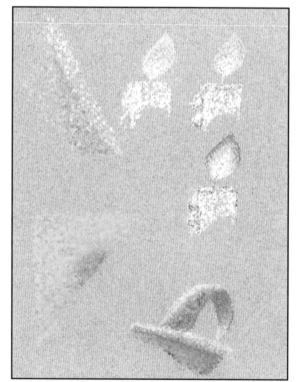

Detail

Stage 2

Stage 3

Demonstration 10
Still Life - Color

If you have tried out the previous demonstrations in this book you will now be starting to understand the nature and possibilities of pastels.

As you know, with pastel sketching, the pastel is not rubbed and blended with the finger as it is in pastel painting. It is applied directly to the paper surface and the background color is allowed to show through to become an integral part of the finished work. Here is an opportunity to use an exciting range of colors and to try the pastel sketching technique on the same still life subject we used in Demonstration 4 when we were experimenting with only black and white pastels.

The subject is a bowl of fruit, a wine bottle and a wineglass on a blue checked tablecloth with a pinkish-mauve drape in the background. The lines of the folds of the hanging drape and the perspective lines of the tablecloth lead our eyes from all four corners of the picture to our main subject on the table.

The bottle gives height to the composition, the bowl of fruit slightly to one side and behind the bottle and the overhanging bananas help to add depth. There is a lively color interest. The light source is coming from the right-hand side.

Stage 1: Use a pink pastel paper and sketch the subject out with a piece of white pastel. Try to ensure that the bottle and wineglass are vertical and do not lean to one side or the other. This can be checked by turning the sketch upside down. Any leaning lines can be checked and corrected as simply as that.

Stage 2: To ensure that you do not smudge what you are sketching, work from top to bottom, left to right if you are right-handed, or right to left, if you are left-handed. Snap a short piece of dark pink pastel and use the long side down to lay in the shadow areas of the folds in the drape. The highlights on the drape can be picked out with pale pink.

Handy Hint: Turn your sketch upside down to check your lines. Lines that are leaning or slanting are easier to see and correct when you look at your sketch upside down.

Stage 1

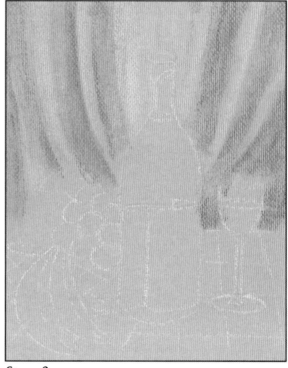

Stage 2

Still Life Detail

Stage 3

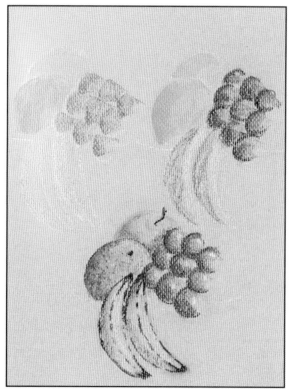

Stage 4

Stage 3: Using medium green, yellow, white and black, build up the wine bottle in the three stages shown. Apply the medium green, then pick out the yellowish-green. For the very dark green area, use green superimposed with black. Use white to pick out the highlights. Using white and medium gray pick out the label shapes. The label details can be added with red, green and black.

Stage 4: The fruit in the glass bowl and the wineglass can be built up in a similar manner. With the fruit, watch especially for the stippling on the orange skin, the dark black ends to the banana, the rich dark shadow and the highlights on the grapes.

Stage 5: When building up the wineglass, the darker red of the wine is made by superimposing black on red. Also emphasise the darkest parts of the wineglass and the sharp white highlights. Finally, add the checked tablecloth, using pale blue for the cloth with a darker blue to draw in the lines of the pattern.

Stage 5

Finished still life

Demonstration 11
Landscape

Landscape subjects provide good material for the pastel artist. The versatility of pastels enables one to capture the changing seasons and express all manner of landscape moods, from gentle atmospheric landscape to the bright colorfulness of a sunset, from a snow-covered landscape to green fields and trees on a warm summer afternoon.

Using the pastel sketching technique, I show how to create a landscape sketch in color on a bluish-gray pastel paper.

Stage 1: You can either choose to lightly sketch out the subject in white pastel, or to work freehand, putting the sky in first and then building up the landscape.

Stage 2: Using the sides of white, then light blue and dark blue pastels, create the sky, leaving parts of the paper showing through.

Stage 3: With the tips of light and medium green pastels and a reddish-brown for the copper beech tree, block in the first stages of light and dark for the trees and bushes. Using medium green, light blue and white pastels with sideways sweeping pastel strokes, start the river, remembering again to leave parts of the paper showing.

Stage 4: With a darker green, pick out the darker tones of the green tree foliage and bushes. Use a darker brown for the copper beech tree foliage and tree trunks. With a dark green and reddish-brown, hint at the reflections of the tall, slim poplar trees and beech tree.

Stage 5: Using the top edge of your pastels complete the tree reflections in the river and add the white highlights on the water. Use a stick of green pastel to draw in the grasses in the foreground corners of the picture. With light brown, dark brown and white draw in the fence entering the river from the left-hand bank.

Stage 1

Stage 2

Stage 3

Stage 4

Stage 5

Demonstration 12
Seascape

Anyone who has stood close to the seashore and witnessed the sounds and color of crashing, swirling waves will almost certainly have been moved or inspired by it. The sea can be a dramatic subject, one which I encourage people to try.

Stage 1: Sketch out the subject with white pastel.

Stage 2: Use white and light blue for the main sky. Superimpose a little dark blue on the darker clouds to the left and right, but keep the horizon quite light. Use pale blue and white for the distant sea and waves beyond the rock. Start the rocks with a cream and a medium brown pastel.

Stage 3: Add a darker brown and then a little black pastel to the rocks. Use light and dark blue, a little black and then white to create the swirling, wavy foreground sea.

Details of stages 2, 3 and 4 can be seen in the detail panel over the page.

Stage 4: The line and detail of the rocks are picked out with the side and tip of a black pastel. The effect of the white sea foam splashing upwards behind the right- and rocks is created by stippling with a white pastel. The white crests of the foreground waves are also added with a white pastel.

Handy Hint: Try to imagine what it would look, sound and feel like standing by this seascape. The sea is constantly moving. You can hear the sounds of the sea crashing against the rock and you can feel the wind. Try to capture that feeling in your picture.

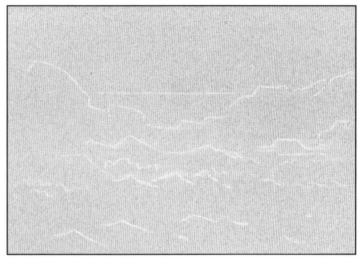

Stage 1

Stage 2

Stage 3

Stage 2   Stage 3   Stage 4

Detail panel

Stage 4

Demonstration 13
Pastel Painting

In the demonstrations so far, we have focussed on *Pastel Sketching*, in which the color of the paper is used as a feature of the sketch. We'll now look at the art of *Pastel Painting*. In *Pastel Painting*, you will use your finger and other tools to smudge and blend the pastels, completely covering the color of the paper, as in the blue ball illustrated on the right.

Stage 1: Draw the ball outline in white pastel. Place light blue, medium blue and dark blue as in the areas shown in the demonstration.

Stage 2: Gently rub and blend the patches of pastel color together using the tip of your finger.

Stage 3: Add the yellow and orange background, again, blending them with your finger. Add the shadow on the table with a little dark brown and black.

Your fingers will become quite messy with color from the pastels, so remember to have a clean, damp cloth in a plastic bag by your side; this will enable you to keep wiping your fingers clean.

Mistakes can be removed and corrections made, by gently jabbing at the surface of the paper with a clean, dry brush to dislodge the loose pastel which you can blow off the picture surface. A clean kneaded eraser can be used to rub away the remaining area of color, which will keep the pastel from smearing.

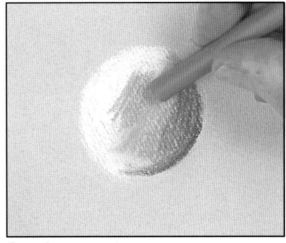
Stage 1

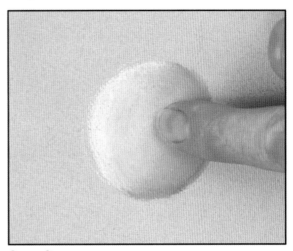
Stage 2

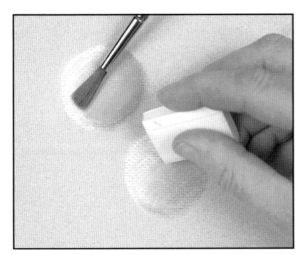
How to brush and then rub away pastel.

Stage 3

Demonstration 14
Landscape

This landscape provides a very good subject to help you quickly understand the technique of blending pastels.

Stage 1: Sketch out the landscape using white pastel on a medium gray paper.

Stage 2: Using pieces of pastel on their sides, create bold strokes of white, medium blue and dark blue for the sky. On the paper, lay sweeping side strokes of gray, blue and mauve for the hills. Apply light sweeping side strokes of medium yellow, light green and medium green pastel for the fields. Using light pressure, superimpose a few white strokes on the green fields, just to give a hint of white. Add darker green patches of pastel on the tree and bush areas. Be generous with the pastel, put lots on the paper.

Stage 3: Go in turn to the sky, hills and fields and gently rub and blend the areas of color with a fingertip, then rub and blend the bushes and trees. Gradually the color will obliterate the background color of the paper and a smoother look than that seen in the pastel sketching technique, should now be observed.

Stage 4: In the finished pastel study, notice how the form and details have been added to all the trees and bushes. A white fence has also been added to the right corner area of the landscape to complete the picture.

Detail: In the detail panel you will see the build-up of stages 1 and 2, and I show how to use a darker green and the top edge of a round or square black pastel to emphasise the line, form and bushiness of the trees and foliage.

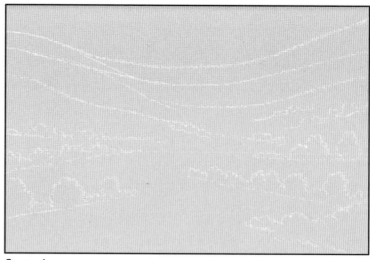

Stage 1

Stage 2

Stage 3

Stage 4

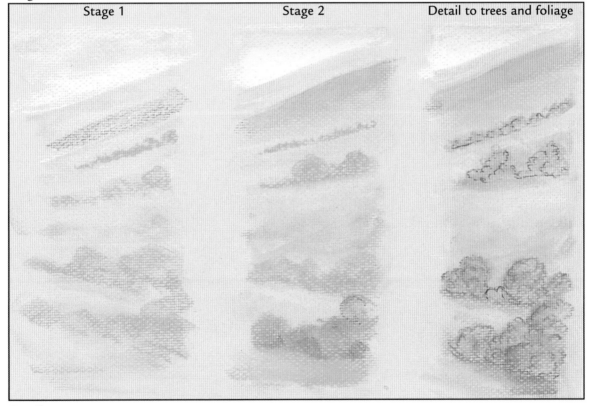

Stage 1   Stage 2   Detail to trees and foliage

Detail

Demonstration 15
A Sunset

The fiery evening sunset takes us into a brighter, more vivid range of colors. Providing some larger areas on which to practice pastel blending, while using a silhouette for detail and contrast between light and dark.

Stage 1: On this occasion, rather than sketch out the subject, create the sunset and reflection in the water first. Use white pastel for the sun, yellow and orange in the remaining areas, with just a little crimson red in all four corners of the page.

Stage 2: Blend the colors with your fingertip working from light to dark: white to yellow to orange to red.

Stage 3: Use the top edge of a black pastel or black pastel pencil, to lightly draw on the real and reflected body of the windmill, house, tree and bushes.

Detail A: In the shapes created by the outline, use diagonal strokes of brown pastel to fill in the silhouette in the sky and its reflection in the river.

Detail B: Press more heavily on the brown pastel and go over the first lines again.

Detail C: Use gentle black diagonal lines over the brown, blending with the tip of a finger or, if you wish, leaving it unblended in these areas.

Stage 4: With a pointed black pastel, or black pastel pencil and a ruler, draw in the windmill sails. A little yellow can be used for highlights and also for the windows on the house. Using dark brown pastel and a black pointed pastel, pick out the boughs and branches of the tree. Use orange for the highlights on the tree. Complete the reflections with horizontal strokes of the pastel to add to the watery effect.

Stage 1

Stage 2

Stage 3

Detail A

Detail B   Detail C

Stage 4

Demonstration 16
Snow Scene

Those of us who live in areas where snow falls in the winter months, enjoy one of nature's great events. We see our familiar landscapes blanketed in white, offering us exciting and new subject possibilities. When the snow has fallen, there is a unique silence which gives the landscape its own special atmosphere. The mauvish - blue and gray shadows play upon the white snowscape, offering the artist very special opportunities.

Stage 1: Sketch out the subject with white pastel on a gray paper.

Stage 2A: (left side) Lay on broad sweeping strokes of white and blue pastel for the sky. Use blue, white and gray pastel for the snow -covered mountains and fields. Use white and gray pastel with a patch of vivid green for the fir trees on the left - hand side.

Stage 2B: (right side) Rub and blend the pastel gently with your finger tip to create the blended effect seen here.

Stage 3: For the central areas use a sharpened black pastel or a black pastel pencil, and the top edge of a brown pastel to pick out the detail of the trees, stone wall, barn and the grasses which peek through the foreground snow.

> **Handy Hint:** Because of the speed with which you can work in pastel, they are excellent for outdoor sketching in cold weather. The sketches can then provide useful material for indoor painting in any medium.

Stage 1 Outline

Stage 2A   Stage 2B

Stage 3

Demonstration 17
Albert Tower

One of my favorite landscapes features the Albert Tower on the Isle of Man. The island sits in the Irish Sea midway between Great Britain and Ireland. The Albert Tower, in the north of the island, was built on high ground overlooking Ramsey Bay, on the spot where Queen Victoria and Prince Albert stood to admire the view on an official visit to the Isle of Man. This unique piece of Victorian architecture now houses high-tech broadcasting antennas and equipment, proving that conservation and technology can go hand in hand.

Stage 1

Stage 1: Sketch out the subject in white pastel.

Stage 2: Block in the main areas of pastel colors for the sky using white, a little light blue and gray. Block in the mountains, hillside and foreground fields, using pale yellowish-greens superimposed with darker greens. Use a brownish-black mix on the shaded left-hand side of the mountains. Block in the light and medium dabs of gray to suggest the stonework for the tower. Add the reddish-browns and cream for the featured stonework on the main tower and for the wood of the door.

Stage 3: Add the stronger medium and darker green tones to the trees and to the foreground grass. Use a black pastel pencil to pick out the detail to the stonework of the tower, wall and trees and foreground grass.

Handy Hint: If sketching or painting out of doors spend 10 to 15 minutes walking around your chosen view or subject as you may find an even better viewpoint. Don't just take the first viewpoint that catches your eye, even though you may choose that in the end.

Detail

Stage 2

Stage 3

Demonstration 18
Bridge over River

"Curved is the line of beauty, straight is the line of duty" is a favorite saying of mine when talking to art students. Much in nature is based on curved lines, circles and ovals, but so much of what man builds is based on straight lines. This subject combines straight and curved lines.

Stage 1: Sketch the outline of the subject in white.

Stage 2: By now you should be familiar with how to mass in the main blocks of color for each area. A tendency people often have is to be skimpy with the amount of pastel they put on the paper, but don't be. With the pastel painting technique you really have to be prepared to use a substantial amount of pastel, especially the lighter colors.

Stage 3: Rub and blend the main areas of pastel so that all the paper is fully covered.

Stage 4: This is where you start to look for and develop the essential features and details: add

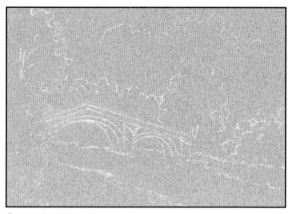

Stage 1

stronger blue to sky and water, add the shadows under the bridge arches, the dark greens and highlights on the foliage, the highlights on the water, the foreground stones and rocks in the river.

Stage 2

Stage 3

Stage 4

43

Demonstration 19
Fruit and Vegetables

The French painter Cézanne once said that all the problems in painting were to be found in a bowl of apples; consequently he drew and painted lots of them. Fruit and vegetables can provide a wealth of material, both for pastel sketching and pastel painting with great diversity of color and surface texture. Many everyday objects we take for granted can often make great subjects. On your next visit to a grocery store or supermarket, look around and think for a moment how you could create pictures from the items you see. It might be a study of a single apple, a selection spread on a table or a more complex grouping.

Handy Hint: When painting fruit, vegetables or flowers which you are going to continue painting the next day, carefully wrap the subjects in polythene bags and place them in a refrigerator. They will retain their freshness longer.

Apple

Mushrooms, tomatoes and carrots

Demonstration 20
Narcissus

In an earlier demonstration I showed a bold, pastel sketch of a sunflower. In this demonstration of the Narcissus, I have used a gentler, pastel painting technique to give a more photographic look.

Stage 1: I want the black paper to provide the background color for the flower to be seen against. Draw the outline shape in white.

Stage 2: Apply white and pale cream pastel for the petals, yellow and orange pastel for the center and medium and light green for the leaf.

Stage 3: Blend the larger areas with your fingertip and the smaller areas with a tortillon or a stub. Apply a dark brown pastel very lightly, then blend the shadows. Use a black pastel for the darker shades and key lines, and gently on the green, then blending it for the darker green shadows on the stem and back of the leaf.

Be prepared for an intriguing surprise when painting potted plants or cut flowers. They will change and alter before your eyes as you paint them. Flowers are living organisms; the time of day, changing light and warmth of the environment affects them, just as those conditions affect us.

Handy Hint: Set light flowers against a dark background and dark flowers against a light background. If working indoors from life, ensure your subject has a good strong light coming from the left or right - hand side, either from a window or from an angled tablelamp.

Demonstration 21
Licorice Allsorts

If ever there was a subject made for pastels, especially the square pastel, it must be licorice allsorts. Open a package, scatter a few on a sheet of paper on the table in front of you and you have a subject in seconds. The square allsorts can be drawn in minutes using the wide side and narrow, top edge of a square pastel. The blue and pink allsorts towards the front of my picture, known as hundreds and thousands, can be captured with stippling. The larger, round allsorts can be created in the pastel painting technique. For the table I used light and medium blue pastels, with black for the shadows and for the licorice. When finished you can enjoy the picture and eat the allsorts!

Detail

Licorice Allsorts

Demonstration 22
Tinting Watercolor Paper for Pastels

Although pastel paper is normally colored, it is also available in white. Exciting possibilities are open to you when using white CP (slightly textured), or 'rough' watercolor paper, as it can be tinted any color or combination of colors, using watercolors or acrylic paint. Suitable white watercolor paper, such as Cotman or Winsor and Newton artist quality paper can be bought by the sheet or in sketch pad form from any art supply shop.

Cut a sheet of the paper to the size you want. Using a strong gummed tape, stick all four sides of the paper to a wooden drawing board. Use a large flat watercolor brush to apply a wash of watercolor or acrylic paint of your choice to the paper. Let it dry naturally, or accelerate the drying by using a hair dryer. Any warping of the paper should go away as it dries flat.

'NOT' watercolor paper

'ROUGH' watercolor paper

Plain white watercolor paper

Tinting watercolor paper for pastels

Composition

The sketch or drawing of your subject, your skill in coloring it, the use of color, light and shade and the illusion of textural effects are all important elements of your painting. Equally important is the composition of your work.

There are certain guidelines that, if followed, can help to build a sound compositional foundation for your work. One important rule is to not have any line or object cut your picture into two equal halves in order to avoid monotony in the composition. Note how in Views A and B below, the views are cut in half horizontally by the horizon and vertically by the tree trunk. By setting the horizon slightly lower (View C) and offsetting the tree trunk to the left of center (View D) the composition becomes much more dynamic and visually interesting.

Focal Points and Key Lines

When looking at your work, the viewer's eyes should not be wandering around the painting as though lost. You are the artist; you are in control, so decide what it is that you want people to be looking at in particular. In other words, your picture should have a FOCAL POINT, or a main feature to which the eyes are led.

In View E, the focal point is the sailboat set in the distance. In View F, it is the village in the far distance, and in View G it is the man standing on the pier in the foreground.

I have arrowed the KEY LINES in each view as well so that you can see how the details in the pictures follow these key lines and lead the viewers eye to the focal points helping to bring the entire composition together.

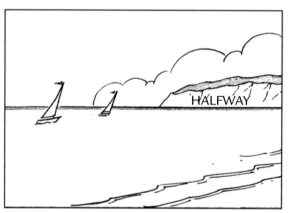

View A

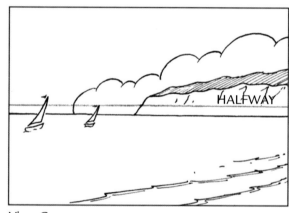

View C

View B

View D

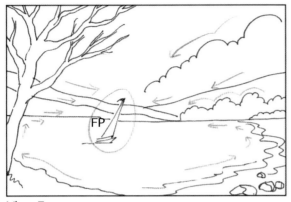

View E

View F

The Triangle

A triangular composition can offer an excellent shape on which to base a painting, especially a landscape, still life or floral study. In the three illustrations, H, I and J, I show this at work. In H, I have created a still life from a vase of flowers and an open magazine. I have placed the vase to the left, forming the left side of the triangle, and the bottom of the magazine form the base of the triangle. In I, the shape of the dish holding the fruit adds to the triangular format of this subject, with the apex just off-center to the right. In J, the figure is seated to the right, forming the upright side of the triangle. The figure's legs under the table help visually form the base of the triangle.

Try to ensure that still life and floral studies have height, width and depth to them.

The next time you have the opportunity to look at paintings or prints by any of the great masters, or even by any fine artist of today, look closely to see how they have employed the important compositional points I have referred to here.

View G

View H

View I

View J

Perspective

The horizon line is an imaginary line across your field of vision when you look straight on; not up or down, but straight ahead. In my sketch you see how the horizon line stays directly in front of the subject regardless if he is sitting down, standing level, or standing higher on a dune. To determine the horizon line when looking at a real subject, hold a ruler by its thin side, horizontally in front of your eyes. This is where the horizon line should be in your composition. Generally, I suggest that you draw the subject lightly first, though, then apply .your horizon line to your sketch. Your horizon line is then used to help apply perspective to the rest of your work and to check and correct your subject.

Perspective is a system of creating the illusion of three dimensions in the objects in your sketch. One way to see perspective in action is to picture the view looking down railroad tracks. The rail ties appear to become smaller and closer together until the tracks merge and disappear.

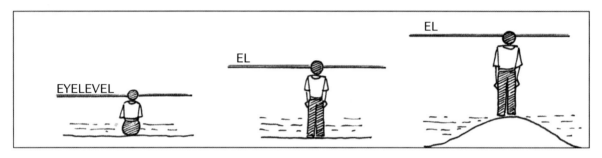

The point where the tracks appear to merge is the "Vanishing Point" (VP), which you will note is a point on the Horizon Line. We know that they don't merge in reality, however by having them vanish on the horizon line we create the illusion that they are getting further away and that the scene has depth.

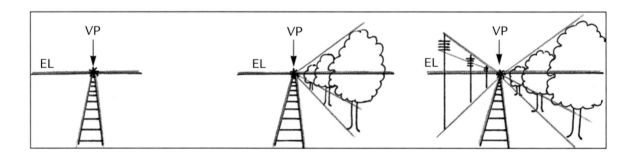

My sketch illustrates this, and I show the tracks with three trees to the right, and then also with telephone poles to the left. Both the trees and the poles appear to become smaller and closer together as they recede. I have shown the guidelines for each item, illustrating how the guidelines all meet at the vanishing point on the horizon line.

Next I show a front view of a picnic basket. With this view, we have just one vanishing point for the top sides of the basket. I am imagining that you or I would be sitting on a chair of similar height when drawing this basket, in which case, I think you would find your eye level would be just about 18" (46cm) above the back of the chair. In my next sketch the basket is set at an angle. We now have vanishing points, one for each side of the basket. Often guidelines want to converge on the eye level, but off the page. This is normal and often happens. When it does, lay scrap paper at the side, tape them

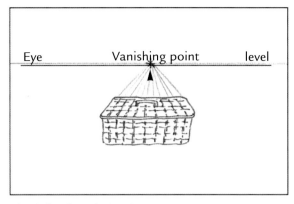

Picnic basket, front view

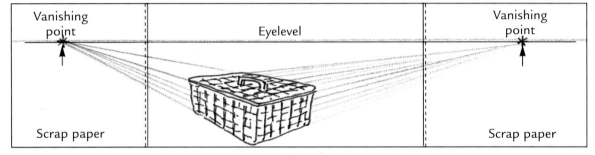

Picnic basket at an angle

on from behind and extend the guidelines onto it in the way I show in my sketch. Never guess or assume the perspective is correct, always try to "prove" it.

Circular perspective

Few people realize that perspective can be used to help solve the problems of drawing circles and ellipses, but it can. I have illustrated this in a sketch of a bowl, a tube, and a rolling pin on its side. I have lightly drawn the group out and placed my eye level well above it. I have then drawn a light guiding square around each ellipse and have drawn those squares in perspective, in the same way the basket was drawn. The squares for the ellipses each have their perspective vanishing points on the common eye level. The bowl and tube share the same vanishing point as their ellipses are on the same plane. The ellipses for rolling pin are on a different plane so they have their own vanishing point at a different position on the eye level. The use of the squares helps determine where each vanishing point should be and ensures the true perspective of the subject where there is an ellipse involved. I then go back to each ellipse and check that it touches the center of each side of the square it occupies, for provided it does, I know that the ellipse must be in perspective. The squares used outside each ellipse and perspective guidelines can be rubbed out gently before a picture is shaded or painted.

Modern Offices at an angle with 2 VPs

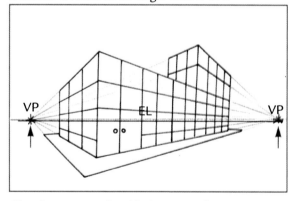

Circular perspective, kitchen utensils

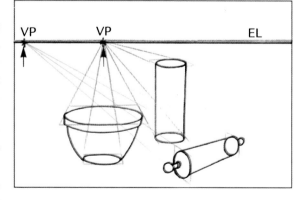

Demonstration 23
Pastel Pencils

Pastel pencils are a very popular way of creating pastel pictures, as they are especially suitable for work in which detail is important. Pastel pencils can be used for a whole range of subjects, and can be combined with the soft pastels used in the previous sections of this book. The pastel comes encased in wood, with a pre-sharpened point, which means that apart from the facility to create detail easily, your fingers will generally remain clean. Although pastel pencils are not included in this kit, it is well worth purchasing a set to experiment with and broaden your skills with pastels.

Below Right: As with all art materials it is important to spend a little time playing with the pastel pencils on some spare paper to see just what effects can be created. Pick up a pastel pencil and try creating the lines and effects you see in the bottom right-hand panel. Try hatching lines, crosshatching, stippling and traditional shading effects working from light to dark.

Opposite: I show a number of other ways to explore the potential of pastel pencils. Note and try the different hatching and crosshatching effects for the colored balls. Draw the outline of the box, then draw it again and shade it in. Make experimental shading strips superimposing one color on another. Note how subtle color changes can be made as the colors overlap. Try creating the tile, brick and tree effects. Try creating the fish silhouettes and face just by using downward hatching lines. Experimenting in this way will be time well spent, as you gain a better understanding of the various effects you can create and how they differ from the same marks made by soft pastels.

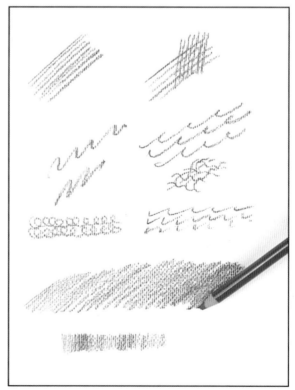

Handy Hint: Do not try sharpening pastel pencils in a pencil sharpener as the tips will often snap off. Use a sharp knife to cut away the wood and then rub the exposed pastel on a sheet of sandpaper to make the point into a round or chisel shape to suit your picture making needs.

Pastel pencil effects for you to try

Demonstration 24
Bread and Cheese

A cut loaf, a piece of cheese and a bread knife are yet another example of how you can create interesting subjects by just looking around your home.

With pastel pencils I have used a hatching technique to sketch this subject.

Stage 1: On a sheet of light gray pastel paper sketch out the subject in white pastel pencil.

Stage 2: Using a light, creamy-beige for the outer bread crust build up diagonal hatching lines. The strength of the tone of color is controlled by the pressure you apply to the pastel. Use the same method for the crust of the slice of bread. Use the light, creamy-beige pastel for the cheese. Show the white bread with white pastel. Hatch in the brown breadboard and knife still using diagonal hatching lines.

Stage 3: Using a reddish-brown pastel pencil, superimpose the warmer tones on the bread crust. Use a combination of gentle light brown and gray strokes to create the shadow side of the cheese. Add darker brown lines on areas of the breadboard, with gentle black lines added on top of the shadows. Use a little gray on parts of the bread. Also use this technique for the slice of bread and the knife.

Stage 4: Pick out the darkest areas and emphasise these. Pay special attention to the texture of the bread crust and white bread areas and the detail on the knife. Do not forget to add the dark shadow under the front edge of the breadboard and the white flashes of highlight on the bread knife.

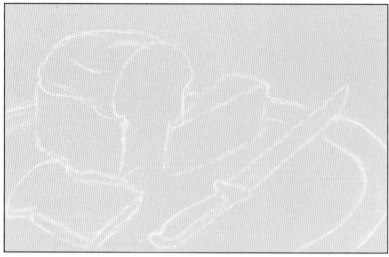
Stage 1

Stage 2

Stage 3

Stage 4

Still life

Demonstration 25
Bird

For this study I used the pastel painting technique. I applied much more of the pastel to each area of the picture, using the pastel pencil to blend the top color into the bottom color. Your finger, a tortillon or a stub can be used for blending. The essential detail was picked out at the end using resharpened pastel pencils.

Stage 1: Draw the bird in white pastel. Start to pastel in the main areas of color.

Stage 2: Look at each area and use darker pastel tones to build up the deeper, darker areas. Use white on the lighter areas, still blending each area to create the lighter and darker tones for the head and body of the bird.

Stage 3: The pastel pencils now enable you to draw in the detail to the eye, beak, feathers and the pattern on the body. The detail on the webbed feet can be added with black pastel pencil.

Opposite page: chalk pastels combined with pastel pencils. For the study of the bottle and glass of Guinness I first created the brown bottle, glass and background using the pastel painting technique with my sticks of soft pastel, blended with my fingers in the manner described earlier in the book. The detail of the bottle labels was easy to add using my pastel pencils.

Stage 1

Stage 2

Stage 3

Demonstration 26
Portrait

The ability to use the sketching or pastel painting technique makes pastels an excellent medium for portraiture. The main blocks of color for the face and hair can be created by blending the colors, while pastel pencils make the addition of details quite easy.

Stage 1: For the study of the young man, sketch the outline in white pastel. Then use generous amounts of red, yellow and white pastel on the face and neck. Likewise, apply light and dark brown to the hair in the way shown.

Stage 2: Blend the pastel strokes of the face and neck with a finger. Shadows to the flesh can be added by superimposing a little strong, deep green and gently blending that into the flesh color to create deeper flesh tones. With a clean finger blend the colors of the hair.

Stage 3: Use the pastel pencils to pick out the detail of the eyes, detail and shadow of the nose, nostril and the lips. The top lip is usually in shadows, so use a darker tone of red. The lower lip catches the light, so add highlights. The lines and contours of the hair can now be added, applying the lighter lines first, then the darker lines.

Stage 4: Add the shirt collar and jacket collar using a blending technique. Use an incomplete sketched look for the rest of the jacket. This will keep the emphasis on the main part of the picture, the face.

Stage 1

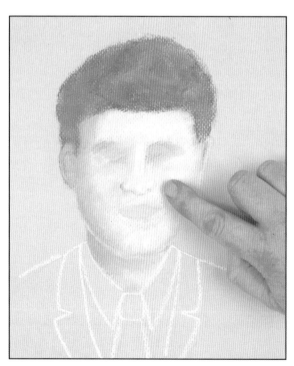

Stage 2

Stage 3

Stage 4

Demonstration 27
Oil Pastels

Oil pastels are very different from chalk pastels and pastel pencils. Because they are oil-based, they will not mix with chalk pastels. They are normally used on their own and have quite different properties from chalk pastels. Most art shops stock both kinds, usually in sets, but sometimes they can be found loose as individual colors.

Both oil and chalk pastels can be used in stick form to draw lines, or to shade in larger areas of color. They can be superimposed on top of one another to create color mixtures and blended effects. Red on yellow will create orange, blue on yellow will create green. Oil pastels, however, can also be blended with a soft sable or synthetic hair brush and turpentine. The artist dips the brush in a little clean turpentine and brushes over the area of oil pastel on the paper to dissolve the paint and blend it, or move it around, in a semifluid state to achieve different effects.

While oil pastels can be used on canvas or canvas board, I find they work best on normal thick cartridge paper. If using turpentine to blend them, a colorless damp stain appears on the paper. This disappears as the turpentine evaporates from the paper.

Opposite page: Here I show the build-up of a banana. With the banana in panel A I used the dry pastel sketching technique. In panel B I used the brush-blended technique. In each example I start with yellow, then add a little green for the shadow and the black for the ends and marks on the skin. Trying these exercises will introduce you to this technique of oil pastels which you can try using other subjects.

Oil pastels

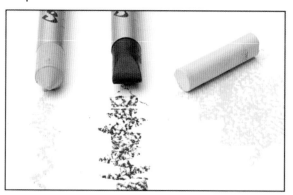

Lines and effects

Blending with turpentine and a brush

Handy Hint: If using a brush for blending, when finished wash the hairs with warm soapy water, cleaning them thoroughly then shake the brush dry. Stand it upright in a jar to enable the hairs to dry completely.

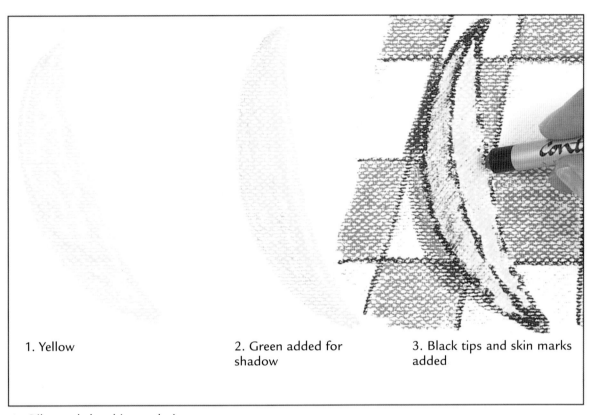

1. Yellow

2. Green added for shadow

3. Black tips and skin marks added

A. Oil pastel sketching technique

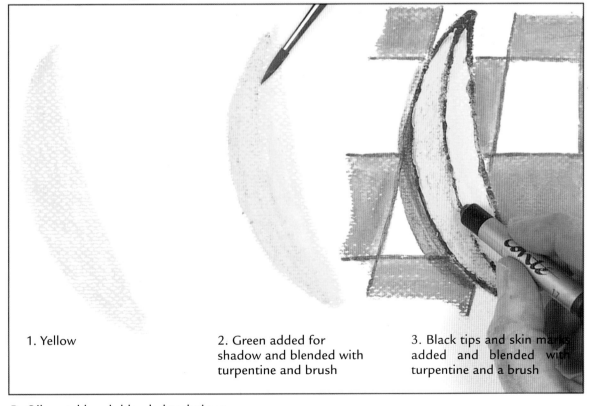

1. Yellow

2. Green added for shadow and blended with turpentine and brush

3. Black tips and skin marks added and blended with turpentine and a brush

B. Oil pastel brush-blended technique

Fixing and Framing Pastels

To prevent pastels from smudging it is a good idea to give each picture a light spray of pastel fixative. Clear fixative is obtainable in ozone-friendly aerosol cans from art stores, but be sure to purchase the correct one for oil pastel versus chalk pastel.

Lay newspaper on a table in a well-ventilated room. Hold the can of fixative 18" (45cm) above the picture and lightly spray it from left to right, top to bottom. Do not over-spray the picture. Any slight dampness will fade as the fixative evaporates. A sheet of acid-free, greaseproof paper can be laid over a dry pastel picture and held in place with paperclips in each corner. This prevents the transfer of color to the backs of other pictures. The finished work can be stored flat in a portfolio.

While some people like to make their own frames, most people take them to a professional picture framer. Pastels are best framed in the same manner as a watercolor. Select a complementary color mat and a suitable frame moulding. A good framer will help and advise you if you ask him or her. The mat provides a border around the picture and an air-space so the glass does not sit on the surface of the picture. A sheet of hardboard is used for the back and the assembled picture is ready for you to hang.

Fixative for pastel pictures.

Backing board, picture, mat, glass and frame before final assembly

Selling And Exhibiting Your Work

You will almost certainly want to keep the first pictures you create for yourself, or give them away as presents to family and friends. But if you have ever walked around an art gallery or have seen paintings for sale, you might, in time, be tempted to try exhibiting and selling some of your own work.

You may be aware of local art galleries where you live. The first thing to do is to find out which have "open" exhibitions. These are shows where any painter can send in one or more original paintings. Normally work will be chosen by a selection committee and you will be notified if yours is accepted or rejected. Some exhibitions will show all work submitted. It is an exhilarating feeling to go to an art gallery and to see work that you have produced hanging in an exhibition. It is also interesting to hear what other people say to one another when they come to a picture you have produced.

Work can often be exhibited and offered for sale in local retail stores such as furniture stores, post offices, shop windows, cafés and restaurants. This usually comes down to you talking to managers and proprietors of such establishments and showing examples of your work. A percentage, from 10% to 33%, is normally requested by an establishment if

An artist viewing her exhibited picture

a picture sells, in return for the display facility. Work can of course be offered for sale in most art exhibitions you enter. If a picture is "not for sale" mark it NFS.

Pricing work can prove tricky and the price will depend on the locality where the work is shown. A good local art gallery director, or picture framer, will often give you guidance, if you ask.

The opening of the annual Southport Palette Club Exhibition

THE FLYING ARTIST'S GUIDE TO

PASTELS

is one of a series of art books which introduce audiences of
all ages to the joy and beauty of artistic creation.

The first four titles in the series are:
The Flying Artist's guide to WATERCOLOR PAINTING
The Flying Artist's guide to OIL PAINTING
The Flying Artist's guide to PASTELS
The Flying Artist's guide to SKETCHING

These titles can be ordered direct from:

Select Publications Ltd.
3918 Kitchener Street
Burnaby, BC Canada
V5C 3M2
Tel: (604) 415-2444
Fax: (604) 415-3444

www.spicebox.ca

Some helpful Do's and Don'ts

1. **Do** play and experiment with your pastels to explore the wide range of marks and effects that can be achieved.

2. **Do** cover the table you are working on with old newspapers.

3. **Do** remember to use a dry paintbrush and a kneeded eraser to dust off and rub away any areas of pastel needing correction.

4. **Do** keep a damp rag in a plastic bag by you to keep wiping your fingers clean.

5. **Do** try round, square and pencil pastels so that you learn the characteristics of each type.

6. **Don't** mix chalk pastels and oil pastels. Use oil pastels separately.

7. **Don't** use too much fixative to spray your pastel picture.

8. **Don't** forget that some of the best subjects are to be found in everyday objects and everyday situations.

9. **Don't** forget to use a mat when framing your pastels under glass.

10. **Don't** let your pastels become damp; store them in a warm room.

* Remember... if you have ever said *"I wish I could paint"* my message to you is

IF YOU WANT TO ... YOU CAN!